Suddenly
Sixty

Also by Judith Viorst
in Large Print:

Forever Fifty and Other
    Negotiations
Murdering Mr. Monti

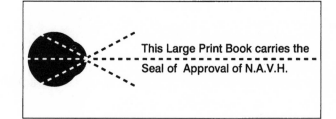

Suddenly Sixty

AND OTHER SHOCKS
OF LATER LIFE

Judith Viorst

Illustrated by Laurie Rosenwald

Thorndike Press • Thorndike, Maine

Published in 2001 by arrangement with
Simon & Schuster Inc.

This book is a work of fiction. Names, characters,
places, and incidents either are products of the
author's imagination or are used fictitiously. Any
resemblance to actual events or locales or persons,
living or dead, is entirely coincidental.

Thorndike Press Large Print Senior Lifestyles Series.

The tree indicium is a trademark of Thorndike Press.

The text of this Large Print edition is unabridged.
Other aspects of the book may vary from the original edition.

Set in 18 pt. Plantin by Elena Picard.

Printed in the United States on permanent paper.

Library of Congress Cataloging-in-Publication Data

Viorst, Judith.
    Suddenly sixty : and other shocks of later life /
Judith Viorst ; illustrated by Laurie Rosenwald.
      p. (large print); cm.
    Originally published: New York : Simon & Schuster, 2000.
      ISBN 0-7862-3247-1 (lg. print : hc : alk. paper)
        1. Humorous poetry, American. 2.Aging — Poetry.
    3. Women — Poetry. 4. Large type books. I. Title.
    PS3572.I6 S8 2001
  811'.54—dc21   2001027022

For Jan Jaffe Kahn
and
Linda Ehren Keninger

Contents

Suddenly Sixty

A Brief History of Marriage

More on Marriage

The Children and Grandchildren

Other Shocks

Suddenly Sixty

It's Harder to Be Frisky
Over Sixty

Inside my shoes and my panty hose
I've painted blue nail polish
    on my toes,
A skirmish in the war that I wage
Against the constraints of my
    current age.
Despite the advent of Medicare,
I will still buy bikini underwear
And scorn the notion that
    seniorhood
Means it's too late to be up
    to no good.
I would if I could.

Don't give me extra time to walk
    down the jetway.
And please don't get up and give
    me your seat on the bus.
I'd rather be engagée than Emeritus,
Though it's harder to be frisky
    over sixty.

I'm not prepared to sign up for
    Elderhostel.
Retirement communities? Save
    your brochures.
I'll keep right on trucking as long as
    my strength endures,
Though it's harder to be frisky
    over sixty.

I'm standing firm against the
    Early Bird Special.
I'm out on the dance floor strutting
    what's left of my stuff.
I'd rather say never say die than
    enough is enough,
Though it's harder to be frisky
    over sixty.

I don't intend to stop showing a
    little cleavage.
Nor do I intend to stop flashing
    a little thigh.

I'm still not too old to give it the
  old college try,
Though it's harder to keep trying,
And it's harder to keep trucking,
And it's harder to be frisky
  over sixty.

The Blissful Couple

They laugh together.
Read together.
Dance together.
Paint together.
Listen to music together.
Walk, holding hands, together.

They love exchanging
Warm
Wet
Mushy
Kisses.

He rushes to greet her,
His arms outstretched,
Joyfully calling her name,
When he sees her arrive.

Who, you are wondering,
Is this blissful couple?
She is his grandma.
He is almost five.

The New Alphabet

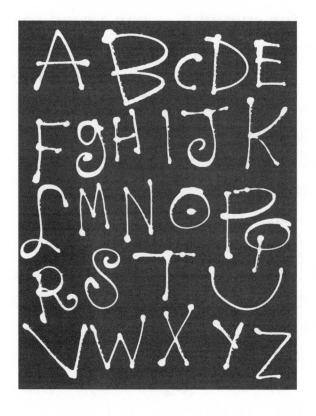

A's for arthritis.
B's for bad back.
C is for chest pains. Corned beef?
 Cardiac?
D is for dental decay and decline.
E is for eyesight — can't read that
 top line.
F is for fissures and fluid retention.
G is for gas (which I'd rather not
 mention)
And other such gastrointestinal
 glitches.
H is high blood pressure.
I is for itches.
J is for joints that are failing to flex.
L's for libido — what's happened to
 sex?
Wait! I forgot about K for bad knee.
(I've got a few gaps in my
 M — memory.)
N's for nerve (pinched) and
 neck (stiff) and neurosis.

O is for osteo-.
P's for -porosis.
Q is for queasiness. Fatal? Just flu?
R is for reflux — one meal
    becomes two.
S is for sleepless nights counting
    my fears.
T is for tinnitus — bells in my ears.
U is for difficulties urinary.
V is for vertigo.
W's worry
About what the X — as in
    X ray — will find.
But though the word "terminal"
    rushes to mind,
I'm proud, as each Y — year —
    goes by, to reveal
A reservoir of undiminished Z — zeal —
For checking the symptoms my
    body's deployed,
And keeping my twenty-six doctors
    employed.

Old Friends

Old friends. We are very old
	friends, as in
We've known each other so long
We knew each other back when we
	were virgins,
Back when we helped each other
	figure out how far to go,
And whether we ought to go there,
	and with whom,
Back when we experimented with
	hating our parents and loving
	de Beauvoir and Sartre,
Back when we talked, with the same
	degree of passionate intensity,
About eyeliner and the meaning of the
	universe.

Old friends, grown up and still
	friends. We exchanged
Our recipes for meat loaf and for
	marriage,

24

And our remedies for when we
  messed them up,
Assuring each other, over the
  phone calls or coffee,
That though we had screamed at
  our children we were basically
  decent mothers,
And that though we had gained
  seven pounds we were basically
  slim,
And that though, at this moment,
  we most sincerely wished to kill
  our husbands, we basically didn't.
And we talked, between the trips to
  the zoo and picketing the White
  House,
About eyeliner and the meaning of
  the universe.

Old friends, no-longer-young friends,
  we held hands

Through the midlife crisis, the dark
   night of the soul,
The jawline dividing, like Gaul, into
   three separate parts,
While we kept reminding each other
   that feeling depressed could be a
   major growth opportunity,
While we kept consulting each other
   on whether we needed a lover, or
   face-lift, or master's degree,
While we kept on asking each other
   whether this was as good as it gets,
And was that good enough?
While we talked, as time speeded up
   and our metabolism slowed down,
About eyeliner and the meaning of the
   universe.

Old friends, now almost-old friends.
   And at last
We see what our mothers meant

When they boringly said, As long as
    you have your health,
Comforting each other when we dealt
    with diminishing hair in our most
    private places,
Competing with each other when we
    bragged of our grandchildren's
    brains and beauty and charm,
Crying with each other in the doctor's
    office when he broke the news.

How am I going to walk in this world
    without talking to my friend
About eyeliner and the meaning of the
    universe?

Now I Lay Me Down to Sleep

If the mattress is hard, but not
    excessively hard,
If the comforter isn't too heavy
    or too light,
If the bottom sheet has been tucked
    in really tight,
If the temperature in the room isn't
    hot or freezing,
If the neighbor's cat isn't mating in
    the front yard,
If the neighbor's kid isn't playing
    acoustic guitar,
If the car alarm doesn't go off in
    the neighbor's car,
If my husband is neither grinding
    his teeth nor wheezing,
If the blackout curtains are keeping
    the bedroom dim,
If I don't get a cramp in my leg or a
    sinus attack,
If I manage to push my ten thousand
    anxieties back,

If I don't think I hear a burglar quietly
creeping,
If two-thirds of the bed isn't occupied
by him,
If at four in the morning the telephone
doesn't ring,
If the *Times* is delivered gently, and no
birds sing,
I might — I just actually might — do
a little sleeping.

A Modest Proposal

A shrewd friend of mine is persuaded
We'd help everybody in need
If we were assured we would lose a
    pound
Each time we performed a good deed.

How swiftly we'd rush to contribute,
How eagerly we'd volunteer,
If giving to others could guarantee
That our waistlines would reappear.

We'd eat, without fear of reprisals,
The foods our scales used to forbid,
Knowing the flab would dissolve from
    our hips
As soon as we tutored a kid,

Or worked to save owls, whales, or
    forests,
Or read to the sick or the blind.
Spurred by the motto "The larger the
    heart,
The smaller will be the behind,"

We'd raise funds to shelter the
   homeless,
Or cure some disease, or stop war.
Seeing our silhouettes narrowing
   down,
We'd yearn to do more, and still more,

Delighted to make the world better
While also achieving thin thighs.
All of us folks who've been watching
   our weight
Would be easy to mobilize

And turn into daily do-gooders
Released from a diet regime
And enjoying a vast sense of
   virtuousness
Along with a lot of whipped cream.

A Whole Other Stage

I've reached the stage where my
lawyer, my broker, my allergist, and
my president are all significantly
younger than I.

I've reached the stage where I recognize,
when I'm buying new living-room
drapes or a new set of dishes, that
they're likely to be the last ones that
I'll ever buy.

And when I'm starting to tell my
friends some really terrific story,
and I ask them whether I've told
them this story before, and no matter
what story I've started to tell, they
say yes,

I know that I have reached a whole
other stage.

I've reached the stage where I find that
most of the spaces I used to park in
are now too small for my car.

I've reached the stage where I'm no

longer able to call myself middle-
aged because that's what my
children are.
And when going to see two movies at
two separate theaters on the same day,
followed by eating a sausage-and-
anchovy pizza, is what I'm
defining as orgiastic excess,
I know that I have reached a whole
other stage.

I've reached the stage where a lot
of the reading I'm doing is at the
market checking salt-free and
fat-free and expiration dates.
I've reached the stage where nobody
bothers to look at my driver's
license when I want to purchase
tickets at senior rates.
And when I'm out of town and I
phone my husband at six a.m.,
and I ring and ring but he doesn't

answer the phone, and my first
thought is not infidelity but cardiac
arrest,
I know that I have reached a whole
other stage.

I've reached the stage where the people
with whom I once discussed Marcel
Proust are discussing inheritance
taxes and living wills.
I've reached the stage where I couldn't
leave my house for twenty-four
hours unaccompanied by eight
different kinds of pills.
And when I have to admit that, offered
the choice, I'd — unhesitatingly —
give up a night of wild rapture with
Denzel Washington for a nice
report on my next bone density test,
I know that I have reached a whole
other stage.

A Brief History
of Marriage

In the Beginning

Though it's hard to believe, we believe
We belong together.
Something has happened to suddenly
   make us complete.
Like Ginger and Fred we believe
We belong together.
Two separate people dancing to one
   single beat.

I like his good mind. And he's kind.
We belong together.
We're finding it easy to squeeze and to
   please and to blend.
Like Nora and Nick we believe
We belong together.
Isn't it swell making love with your
   very best friend.

He admires my smile. And my style.
We belong together.
In spring we'll be ready to bring on the
   rings and the rice.

Like Adam and Eve we believe
We belong together.
A match made in heaven. A life lived
  in paradise.

A life lived — at least for a while —
  in paradise.

After a While

Though it's hard to believe, it is hard
To belong together.
Something that used to seem
boundless is starting to shrink.
Like sloppy and neat it is hard
To belong together.
How in God's name do two people
share one single sink?

All his jokes are too long. It is hard
To belong together.
We get into bed and already I'm
dreading his snore.
Like surly and sweet it is hard
To belong together.
What are his jockey shorts doing in my
dresser drawer?

Must he gloat when I'm wrong? It is
hard
To belong together.

48

He says that I'm sometimes a pill,
   sometimes shrill. Is that nice?
Like a pair of left feet, it is hard
To belong together.
Oh, where is my Adam? What
   happened to paradise?

Won't someone please tell me what
   happened to paradise?

ntinued

Though it's hard to belong, we believe
We belong together.
There's something between us that's
    stronger than all of the strains.
For better or worse we believe
We belong together.
And sometimes it's stardust, and
    sometimes it's stopped-up drains.

It's been far from ideal, yet we feel
We belong together.
In spite of the tears and tough years
    we've done more than make do.
In sickness and health we believe
We belong together.
And sometimes it's skylarks, and
    sometimes it's stomach flu.

Perfect match? We were wrong.
    Nonetheless,
We belong together.

We're counting on laughter and trust,
   and some lust, to suffice
Till death do us part. We believe
We belong together.
This may be the closest it gets
   to paradise.

And sometimes we still get a
   glimpse of paradise.

More on Marriage

So My Husband and I Decided to Take a Car Trip Through New England

Even if I had a Ph.D. in psychology,
Even if I were a diplomatic whiz,
Even if I were Queen of the Charmers
  and more irresistibly sexual
Than whoever the current reigning
  sexpot is,
And even if I had a fortune to
  squander on payoffs,
And even if I had Mafia connections,
It still would be impossible to
  persuade my husband, when lost,
To stop — please stop — the car,
  and ask for directions.

Even if I were collapsing from thirst
  and from hunger,
Even if I were reduced to darkest
  gloom,
Even if I observed, between sobs, that
  we should have arrived three hours
  ago,

And the inn was going to give away
   our room,
And even if I revived all my marital
   grievances:
Old hurts and humiliations and
   rejections,
It still would be impossible to
   persuade my husband, when lost,
To stop — just stop — the car,
   and ask for directions.

Even if I were to throw a full-scale
   temper tantrum,
Even if I were to call him an uncouth
   name,
Even if I were to not-so-gently suggest
   that should we wind up getting
   divorced,
He would have nobody else but
   himself to blame,
And even if I, in a tone I concede is
   called screaming,

Enumerated his countless
    imperfections,
It still would be impossible to
    persuade my husband, when lost,
To stop the goddamn car,
    and ask for directions.

A Very Very Brief History of Marriage

1963 — Niagara.
1999 — Viagra.

In Response to a Request for an Apology

I've read that the ability to apologize is one of the hallmarks of a mature marriage.

I didn't say it.

I didn't do it.

You wouldn't want me to lie and
accept the blame for something I'm
not guilty of.

I believe I'm a big enough person to
concede that I've been wrong when
I've been wrong.

But I wasn't, and therefore I won't —
not even for love.

I won't admit it.

I can't admit it.

I know it isn't my fault and, if it is,
may God — this moment! —
strike me down dead.

I'd gladly say I'm sorry except
there's nothing for me to say I'm
sorry *for*.

Okay, I'll take back *how* I said it, but
not *what* I said.

They made me do it.
They drove me to it.
In view of all these pressures and
  provocations how could I have done
  otherwise?
But if you are willing to grant
That I can't be held completely
  responsible,
And that there are plenty of others
  who share the blame,
And that you're also fallible,
And that you've made mistakes,
And that, if you'd been me,
  you'd have done the same,
And if you are willing to promise
That you'll never throw it up to me,
And that I won't look lesser in your eyes,
Then maybe I'd be willing,
I'd probably be willing,
I guess I'm willing to
Apologize.

Anniversary Dinner

Whatever it is
That teases the palate,
Amuses the bouche,
Fizzes the champagne,
Puts the voilà in foie gras,
Sizzles the châteaubriand,
Lifts the soufflé,
And makes of this dinner
A bit of heaven on earth,
Makes you the favorite meal
Of this gourmet.

About His Retirement

He's pointing out where I left some
  dust on the baseboards.
He's watching out for which foods I
  am letting go bad.
He's giving me guidance on how to
  water the houseplants.
He says that I ought to be glad.
  I am not glad.

He's nudging me when I fail to floss
  after mealtime.
He's alerting me when I gain even half
  a pound.
He's pestering me to straighten my
  spine and stop slouching
Whenever he's around. He is always
  around.

He's starting conversations with me
  when I'm reading.
He's chiming in when I talk with my

friends on the phone.
He's coming with me when I shop at
the supermarket
So I won't have to shop alone. I like
alone.

He's sitting beside me while I'm
tweezing my eyebrows.
He's standing beside me while I'm
blow-drying my hair.
He's sharing those moments when I
am clipping my toenails.
You want my opinion? He's overdoing
share.

He's keeping track of how I am
spending each second.
He also keeps track of how much I
spend on my clothes.
Before he retired I told him he must
find a hobby.
Now he's retired. And guess who's the
hobby he chose?

A Wedding Sonnet
for the Next Generation

He might compare you to a summer's
    day,
Declaring you're far fairer in his eyes.
She might, with depth and breadth
    and many sighs,
Count all the ways she loves you,
    way by way.

He might say when you're old and
    full of sleep,
He'll cherish still the Pilgrim soul
    in you.
She might — oh, there are poems so
    fine, so true,

74

To help you speak of love and vows to
   keep.

Words help. And you are writing your
   own poem.
It doesn't always scan or always
   rhyme.
It mingles images of the sublime
With plainer words:
   Respect. Trust. Comfort. Home.

How very rich is love's vocabulary
When friends, dear friends,
   best friends decide to marry.

The Children and Grandchildren

Just a Few Words of Advice,
Just a Few Helpful Hints

So your son has announced that he's
    going to marry that woman.
You know he'll be making the biggest
    mistake of his life.
For a daughter-in-law even Lady
    Macbeth deserves better.
And even a Henry the Eighth should
    be spared such a wife.
So before you begin to arrange the
    rehearsal dinner
From cocktails to capons to
    chocolate-covered mints,
You intend (without being critical) to
    (diplomatically) offer him
Just a few words of advice, just a few
    helpful hints.

So your daughter is leaving a job with
    an excellent future.
She's pulling up roots and she's
    moving out West to create,

Unencumbered by furniture, money,
   or health insurance.
This is surely a game plan any sane
   person would hate.
So before she trades in her office and
   East Side apartment
For wind chimes, a futon, and maybe
   some cactus prints,
You intend (without seeming skeptical)
   to (quite respectfully) offer her
Just a few words of advice, just a few
   helpful hints.

So the parents of your new grandchild
   are spoiling him rotten.
He's never heard "no" or "say please"
   or "don't do that again."
It looks like he's worn the same shirt
   from last May through November.
It looks like he's going to breast-feed
   until he is ten.

So before his mother and father are
    too late to stop him
From growing up to be someone
    who'll make the world wince,
You intend (without sounding horrified)
    to (very tactfully) offer them
Just a few words of advice, just a few
    helpful hints.

So our daughters and sons and their
    spouses are no longer children.
They reach their decisions without
    ever calling us first.
They often unreasonably tend to look
    on the bright side,
While we're always asking ourselves,
    What if worse comes to worst?
So before they do something too fatal
    we will rush in with
Anything from a big hug to a check to
    a blintz,

In addition to which we'll continue
  to(oh-so-unintrusively) offer them
Just a few words of advice, just a few
  helpful hints.

Did I Do Something Wrong?

Quality time and vitamin C and a
    book before bedtime at night,
I did everything right.
Then why, when I reach out to touch
    him, does he hold me at bay?
Something inside of me dies
When I look in my son's shuttered
    eyes,
So far from here. So very far away.

Tricking and treating and soccer
    games and the second grade's
    Halloween show,
I was sure to go.
And yet he is stumbling through
    jungles of bitterest black,
Lost in the fog that he buys,
Wearing a rebel's disguise,
Unwilling, or unable, to come back.

I never claimed to be the perfect
   mother.
I made mistakes. Well, everybody
   did.
But God, I was so glad to be his
   mother.
And God, oh God, oh God,
   I loved this kid.
I love this kid.

Patience and laughter and trips to
   the beach and tickles and song,
Did I do something wrong?
Am I kidding myself? Am I simply
   rewriting the poem?
Telling myself a few lies,
While somewhere a frightened child
   cries,
And I wait, and I hope, and I pray that
   he'll find his way home.

Our Wonderful Annual
Full-Fledged Family Vacation

It is August at the Cape,
And we're here once more
On our wonderful annual full-fledged
    family vacation,
Having taken (for a rent in the low five
    figures) a house large enough to
    accommodate
Our children, their spouses, the
    grandchildren, the two of us, my
    divorced sister-in-law,
And her overenthusiastic Golden
    Retriever,
Without whom, she made clear,
She'd rather not come.

No pets accompanied the families
    flown in by us
(For fares in the low five figures)
From Chicago, Jacksonville, and
    Austin.
And now we are here,

together again for two weeks,
On our wonderful annual full-fledged
   family vacation,

Where I am trying, with moderate
   success, to overlook
The wet beach towels soaking into the
   living-room chairs,
The use of the kitchen table as the
   baby's changing table,
My sister-in-law's chartreuse thong
   bathing suit,
And where I am trying, with moderate
   success, to make pleasing meals
For the one who won't eat anything
   that once had a face,
For the one who won't eat anything
   that is green or swims,
For the one who won't eat anything
   unorganically grown,
For the one who won't eat anything,
And where I am trying, with

moderate success, to find happy
ways to parcel out
The car, a quart of Cherry Garcia ice
cream, and my complete attention
Among adult siblings whose rivalries
always return,
Unresolved, unrepressed, and
untarnished by the years,
On our wonderful annual full-fledged
family vacation.

I am, presumably, having a wonderful
time,
Even though the organic daughter-
in-law and the monthly pedicure
daughter-in-law are not invariably
en rapport
Or on speaking terms,
And even though my husband and I
cannot have sex for two weeks
Because nobody knocks at our
bedroom door before entering,

And even though the grandchildren
  and the Golden Retriever
Have done many irreparable things to
  our rented house,
For which there are sure to be
  penalties
In the low five figures.

This morning I woke up early
And, amid the smell of sweaty
  sneakers and bluefish,
I found myself thinking that maybe
  just *one* week in August,
Or maybe, now that I'm thinking such
  thoughts, just one weekend,
Might make for an equally wonderful,
And perhaps an even more wonderful,
Wonderful annual full-fledged family
  vacation.

When I Watch

When I watch my oldest son
With his little daughter,
Reading her books,
Or patiently braiding her hair,
Or waiting while she chooses, and
    changes her mind, and chooses, and
    changes her mind about
What she will wear,
And when I watch him bathing her,
Or kissing a bump on her forehead to
    make it better,
Or tenderly tucking her into bed at
    night,
I know that, though I did a lot of
    things wrong,
I must have done a few things right.

Being a Grandparent Is
the Best Revenge

You laughed when I worried about
   you. Now
You have a child,
And his merest mosquito bite can
   cause you alarm,
But he laughs when you count the
   ways he could come to harm
Without your protection.

You squirmed when I snuggled with
   you. Now
You have a child,
And you're trying to give him a cuddle
   and a kiss,
But he slips from your grasp,
   determined to resist this
Annoying affection.

You spurned meals I made just for
   you. Now
You have a child,
And you've gone out and bought his
   favorite chicken parts,

But he tells you he's finished — one
    taste after he starts,
Though they're broiled to perfection.

You sighed when I said just you
    wait until
You have a child.
Now I'm here to assure you,
    unequivocably,
That though he is doing to you what
    you did to me,
He's not into rejection.

For he may not want your protection.
And he may not want your cuddles.
And he may not want your chicken.
But he wants mine.

The Sweetest of Nights
and the Finest of Days
A song for our children

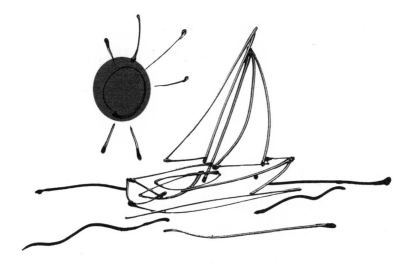

and our children's children

I wish you, I wish you,
I wish you these wishes:
Cool drinks in your glasses.
Warm food in your dishes.
People to nourish and cherish and
    love you.
A lamp in the window to light your
    way home in the haze.
I wish you the sweetest of nights
And the finest of days.

I wish you, I wish you
A talent for living.
Delight in the getting.
Delight in the giving.
A song in your soul, and someone to
    hear it.
The wisdom to find the right path
    when you're lost in a maze.
I wish you the sweetest of nights

And the finest of days.
   A snug roof above you.
   A strong self inside you.
   The courage to go where you
      know you must go,
   And a good heart to guide you.
   And good friends beside you.

I wish you, I wish you
A dream worth the doing.
And fortune's face smiling
On all you're pursuing.
And pleasures that far far
Outweigh your small sorrows.
Arms opened wide to embrace your
   tomorrows.
A long sunlit sail on the bluest and
   smoothest of bays.
I wish you the sweetest of nights
And the finest of days.

Other Shocks

When Asked If I Thought That I'd Finally Got It Together

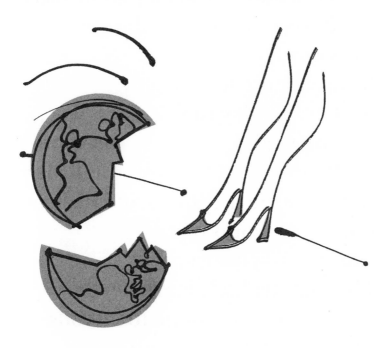

I had it together on Sunday.
By Monday at noon it had cracked.
On Tuesday debris
Was descending on me.
And by Wednesday no part was intact.
On Thursday I picked up some pieces.
On Friday I picked up the rest.
By Saturday, late,
It was almost set straight.
And on Sunday the world was
    impressed
With how well I had got it together.
But spare me the cheers and applause,
For as the world turns
Every sixty-plus learns
That among life's immutable laws
Is one that we're bound to be bound to
Right through to the end of our days:
That although we may get it together,
Together is not how it stays.

Late Love

He dies.
She dies.
And after great loneliness
Those who are left behind
Find each other,
Or redefine each other
From neighbor or old friend
To companion,
Intimate,
And, most amazingly,
Lover.

Their middle-aged children
Sulk,
Saying, without saying it,
This is unseemly.
Devote yourself
To good works,
Educational cruises,
Your grandchildren,
And do not abandon

Your lost mate,
Your past life,
Or us.

Those who are left behind
Turn to each other,
Their soft used flesh
Renewed in a forgiving embrace.
And in their hearts
Such gratitude.
Such gratitude.

To a Husband Who, After
Forty-two Years, Dumped My
Wonderful Friend for a
Much Younger Woman

May you lose your state lottery ticket
the day that you win it.
May each meal that you eat leave a
permanent stain on your clothes.
May you get unsolicited telephone
calls once a minute.
May a large air-conditioning unit fall
down on your toes.
May all of the hair you possess grow
out of your nose.
When you zip up your pants may your
zipper get stuck with you in it.

May you look in the mirror and
shudder at what you are seeing.
May your doctor prescribe
colonoscopies ten times a year.
May your high school reunion class
vote you Least Loved Human Being.
May your chest get so droopy you
need to go buy a brassiere.

114

May your days possess all the
   vibrancy of warm beer.
And throughout every night may you
   do far less sleeping than peeing.

May your license expire and you flunk
   the exam to renew it.
May your dirtiest deeds be exposed in
   the national press.
May you find yourself trying to do it
   much more than you do it.
May the answer to all of your prayers
   be a "no," not a "yes."
May you always be audited by the
   IRS.
And whenever you audit your life may
   you know that you blew it.

Cemeteries and Other Plots

The plan was to go on the ultimate
double date,
Buy resting places for four in a
charming location.
We thought of it as a very extended
vacation,
For which we'd pay well in advance
so as not to be late
And miss being able to pick from the
widest selection
Of tombs with a view, on a hill, in the
shade of a tree.
What a sensible foursome we are,
although secretly
(While we've given a great deal of
thought to how we would choose
them)
None of us believe that we'll ever use
them.

A Thoroughly Modern Sixty

I'm slogging along down the
information highway.
I'd rather read Yeats than my
computer screen,
But I'm told that I cannot survive the
twenty-first century
Unless I can manage to master this
machine,
Which, I have also been told, does not
really hate me,
In spite of the many hostile things it
does.
I aspire to being a thoroughly modern
sixty,
But sometimes I don't like what is as
much as what was.

I'm listening to a recorded menu of
options
And suddenly my brain is turning to
mush.
Do I want my prescription refilled or
departures to Denver?

And when I decide this, which buttons
    do I push?
And why can't the calls I'm making
    simply be answered
By living breathing human women
    and men?
I aspire to being a thoroughly modern
    sixty,
But sometimes I don't like right now
    as much as back then.

I've just returned from a restful
    ten-day vacation.
One hour later I'm needing ten days
    more,
What with voice mail and E-mail and
    faxes demanding attention,
Plus all those FedExes delivered to my
    door.
Next year, I've been told, I should
    travel with a cell phone,
So everyone can reach me faster than
    fast.

I aspire to being a thoroughly modern
    sixty,
But sometimes I don't like the present
    as much as the past.

In order to be a thoroughly modern
    sixty
I'll learn to embrace the new
    technology
By conversing with virtual rather than
    actual people
And reordering pills by pressing
    button three.
I'll never leave home without my
    modem and pager,
Remaining in touch with all who so
    desire.
I aspire to being a thoroughly modern
    sixty,
But sometimes I don't like the sixty to
    which I aspire.

Mortal Question

I didn't know I wasn't there.
I will not know I'm not.
Between these two oblivions
My life unfolds its plot.

I missed the glory that was Greece.
I missed Rome's rise and fall.
My absence from these grand events
Disturbed me not at all.

Nor did I feel deprived because
They held the Renaissance
Some centuries before my birth.
No pre-existence wants

Imposed themselves upon my peace.
Why does some future spring
Collapse my heart with longing when
I will not feel a thing?

Just Lucky I Guess

I've been noticing lately that when I complain about something bad that has happened to me, the person to whom I'm complaining tells me how fortunate I am that it wasn't much worse.

When my plane lost two engines and
    had to go back to the airport,
They said I was lucky the plane hadn't
    crashed and burned.
When a mugger, at gunpoint, took
    both of my rings and my wallet,
They said I was lucky my credit cards
    were returned.
And when lightning demolished our
    tree, which fell on our house and
    then plunged through our roof and
    into our bedroom,
They said I was lucky I wasn't home at
    the time.
Why does this happen to me? I'm
Just lucky I guess.

When my luggage was lost for three
    days on our trip to Bermuda,
They said I was lucky it wasn't a
    dress-up trip.
When I slipped on an ice patch and
    broke my right foot in two places,

They said I was lucky I hadn't broken
   my hip.
And when my cousin, the klutz,
   somehow managed to spill an entire
   carafe of Merlot on my carpet,
They said I was lucky my sofa escaped
   the spray.
Why does this happen to me? Hey,
Just lucky I guess.

When the caterer canceled and forty
   were coming for dinner,
They said I was lucky I'd saved the
   catering fee.
When I looked at the glass and I saw
   that the glass was half empty,
They said I was lucky I still was able to
   see.
And when my least favorite aunt
   became ill while visiting me this past
   March, and stayed on till September,
They said I was lucky she left before
   the next snow.

Why does this happen to me? Oh,
Just lucky I guess.

When somebody smashes my Chevy
  but leaves me unmangled,
I know that I ought to be grateful
  rather than curse.
When my endodontist performs root
  canal on my molars,
I know that I must keep in mind that it
  could have been worse.
And I know I should thank my good
  fortune, when disease or disaster
  strikes,
That my troubles are nothing
  compared to hers or his,
But I'm tired of telling myself that
  the answer to
Why does this happen to me is
Just lucky I guess.

If Only

If only shopping at Saks counted as
exercise.
If only aggravation made me thin.
If only there was a pill I could take for
grace under pressure and upper-arm
definition.
If only I lost as adorably as I win.

If only having insomnia gave me
courage.
If only eating chocolate made me
smart.
If only there was a cloth that washed
off lipstick, mascara, eyeliner,
blusher, and wrinkles.
If only my breasts and my waist were
farther apart.

If only going to movies lowered
cholesterol.
If only constipation made me rich.

If only there was a shot that would
  immunize me against impatience
  and feeling guilty.
If only I laughed as easily as I bitch.

If only French fried potatoes helped
  me remember.
If only they sometimes also helped me
  forget.
If only one morning I'd leap out of bed
  feeling ready and willing and eager
  to welcome old age.
But not yet.
Not yet.
Not yet.
But not quite yet.

The employees of Thorndike Press hope you have enjoyed this Large Print book. All our Large Print titles are designed for easy reading, and all our books are made to last. Other Thorndike Press Large Print books are available at your library, through selected bookstores, or directly from us.

For information about titles, please call:

(800) 223-1244
(800) 223-6121

To share your comments, please write:

Publisher
Thorndike Press
P.O. Box 159
Thorndike, Maine 04986